Easter
Adventure

Activity Book for Kids
Ages 4-8

Bunny & Bear PRESS

- BLANK PAGE -
left for bleed through

Hi there!

Welcome to the Easter world
of cute Bunny family.

The book you have in your hands is
a book full of adventures with cute Bunny
family. They need your help with
getting ready for Easter.

Are you ready to help them?

☐ Let's start
that adventure!   ☐ Yeeeeees!

- BLANK PAGE -
left for bleed through

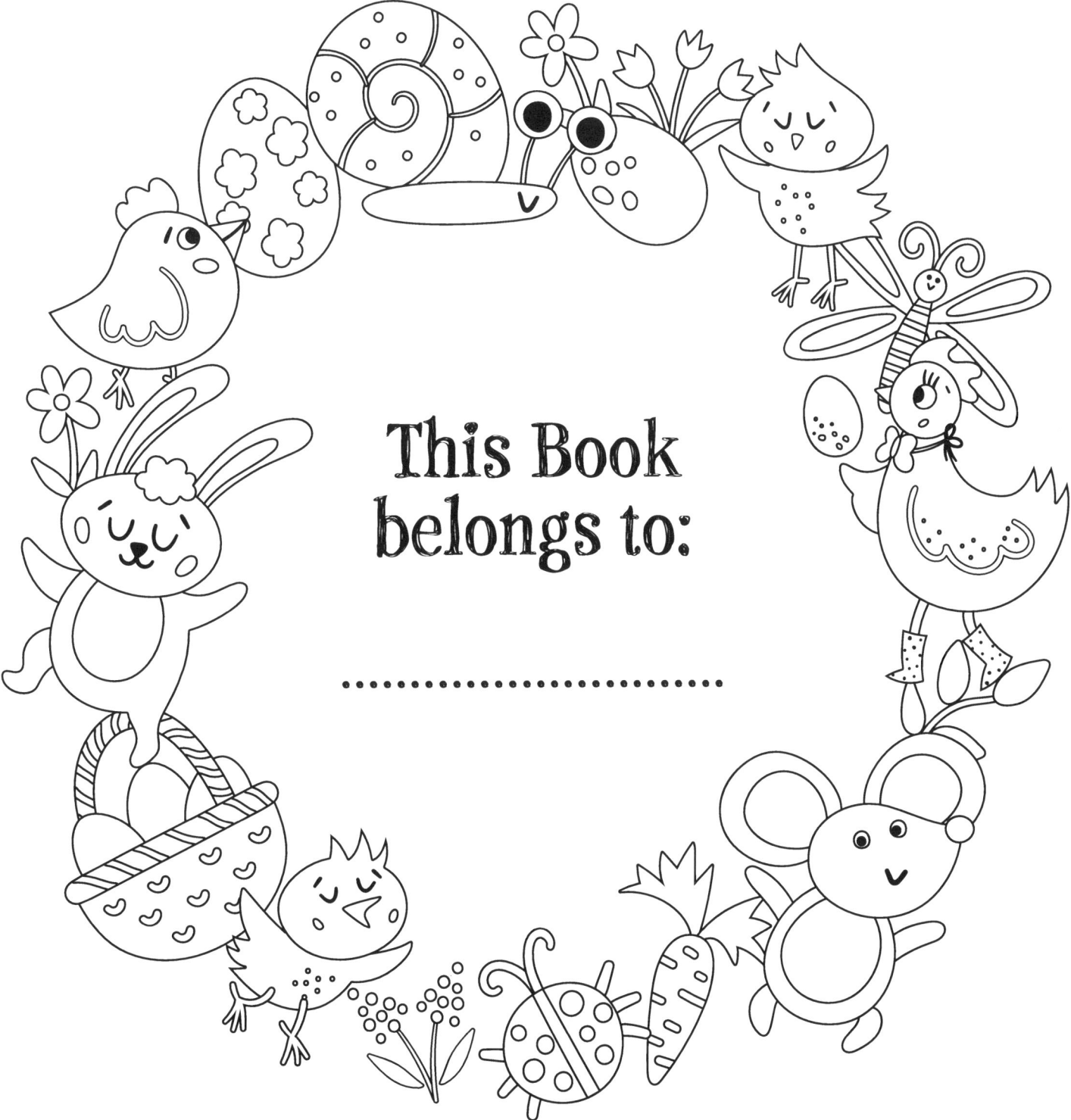

This Book
belongs to:

....

- BLANK PAGE -
left for bleed through

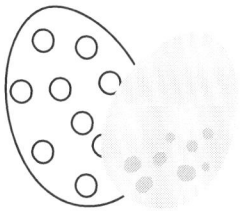

Find the Diffrences

Find and circle 5 diffrences between the pictures.

- BLANK PAGE -
left for bleed through

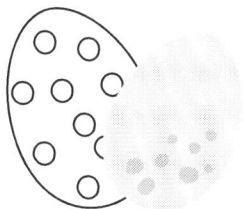

Easter Addition

Count, add and write the total number of eggs.

$$3 + 2 = \boxed{?}$$

$$3 + 3 = \boxed{?}$$

$$4 + 5 = \boxed{?}$$

$$1 + 4 = \boxed{?}$$

$$5 + 2 = \boxed{?}$$

$$6 + 2 = \boxed{?}$$

- BLANK PAGE -
left for bleed through

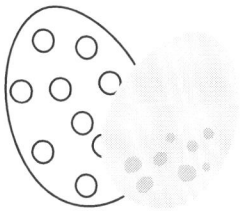

Shadow Matching

Draw a line from each object to its matching shadow.

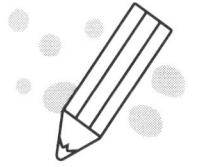

- BLANK PAGE -
left for bleed through

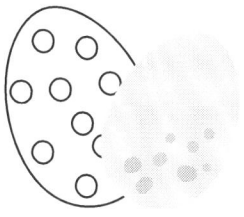

Counting & Matching

Count the objects and write the numbers.
Match the items that are the same.

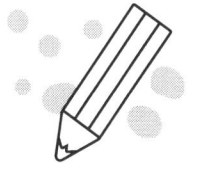

- BLANK PAGE -
left for bleed through

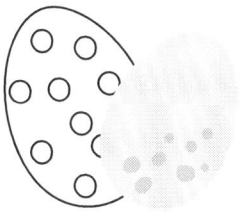

Same

Match the eggs that are the same.

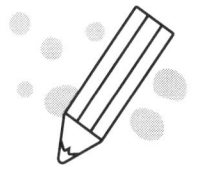

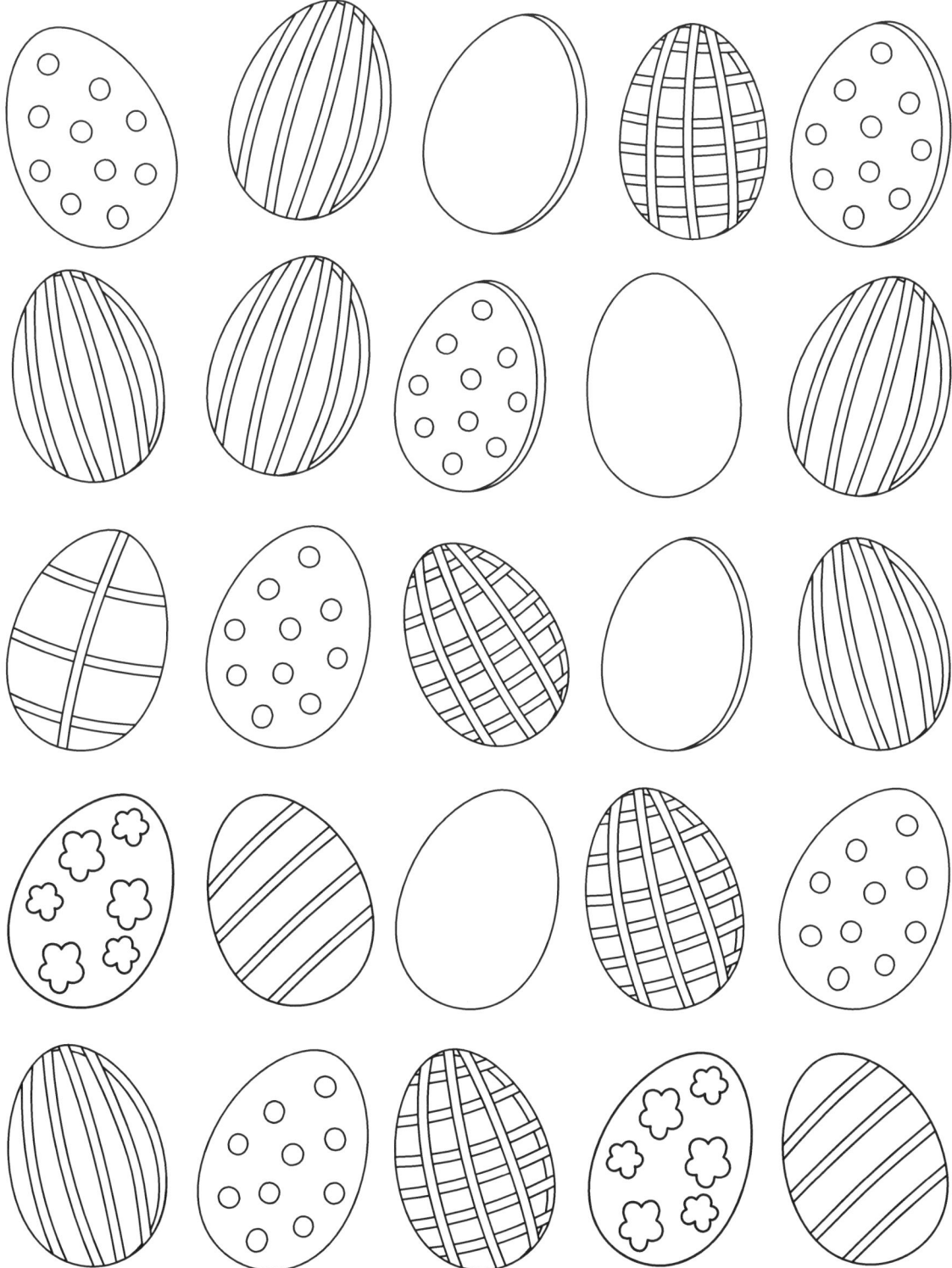

- BLANK PAGE -
left for bleed through

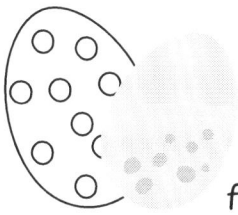

Easter Crossword

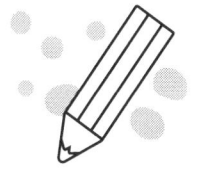

Fill in the crossword grid with the name of each item
following the number and direction indicated. Color the pictures.

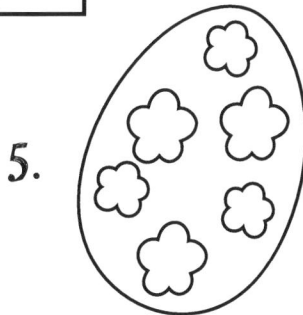

→2.

3.

↓2.

4.

3

2

4

1

5

1.

5.

- BLANK PAGE -
left for bleed through

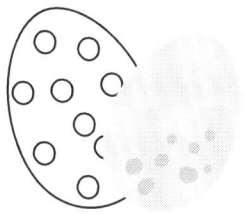

Finish the Picture

Finish drawing the picture. Color the picture.

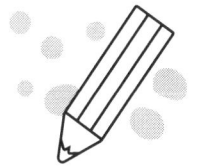

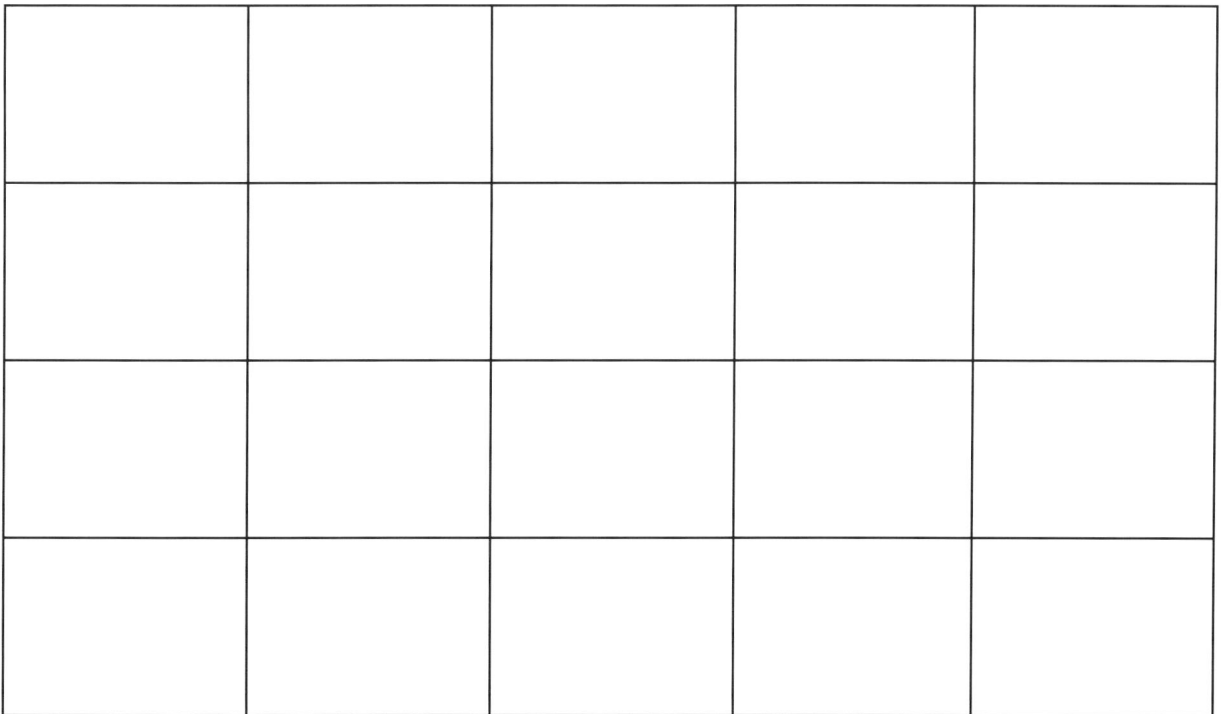

- BLANK PAGE -
left for bleed through

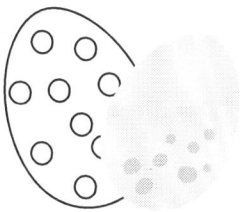

Connect the Dots

Connect the dots. Color the picture.

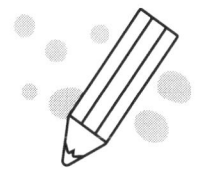

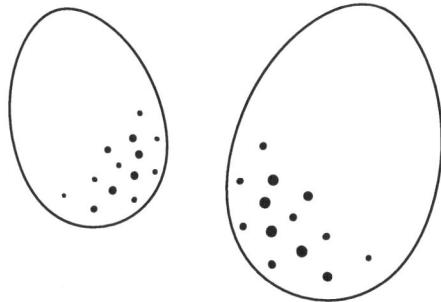

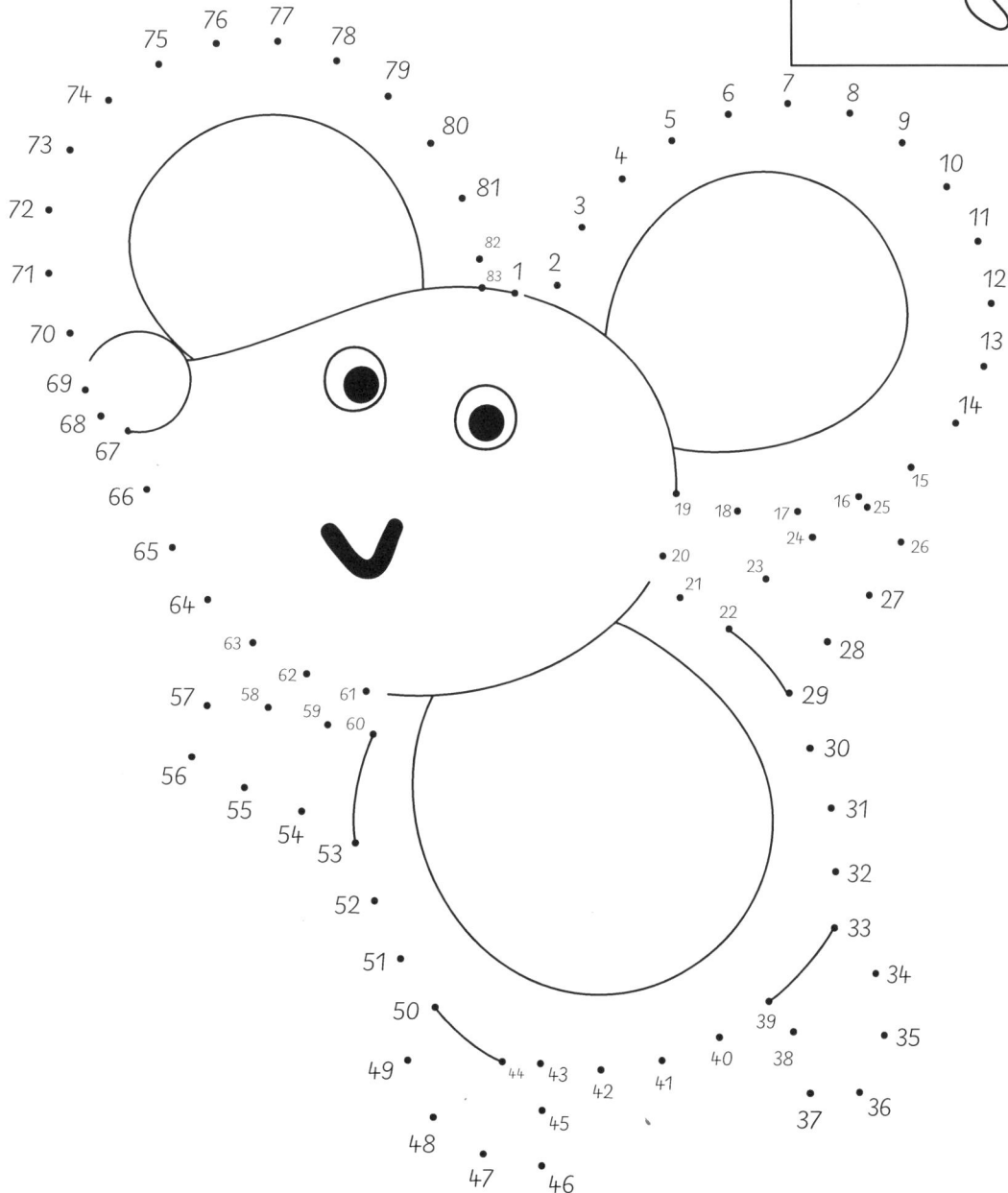

- BLANK PAGE -
left for bleed through

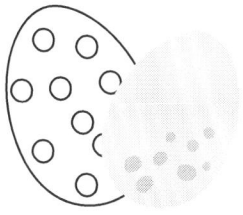

Easter Addition

Count, add, follow the path and write
the total number of eggs.

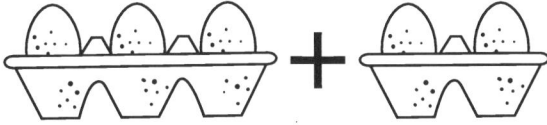

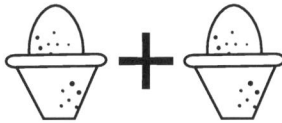

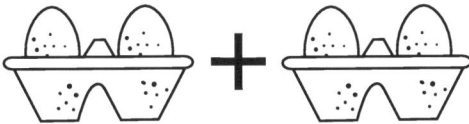

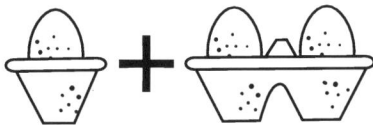

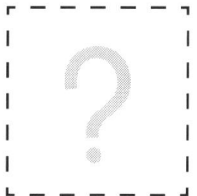

- BLANK PAGE -
left for bleed through

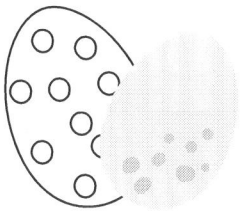

Hidden Objects

Find 10 eggs hidden in the garden.

- BLANK PAGE -
left for bleed through

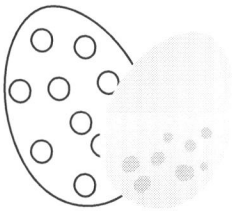

Color, Cut & Paste

Color the pictures. Cut and paste them on the matching place.

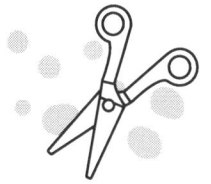

EASTER MARKET

- BLANK PAGE -
left for bleed through

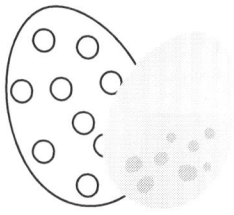

Counting

Draw the line from 1 to 10 to help Baby Bunny get to the Easter basket.

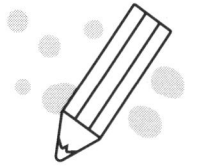

2	7	8	1	2
9	3	6	9	10
8	1	9	5	4	6
	5	2	3	10	4
	1	9	8	6	7

- BLANK PAGE -
left for bleed through

Matching the Numbers

Count eggs in the baskets, match them with the right number.
Match number with eggs.

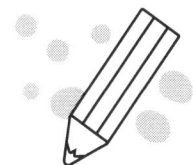

4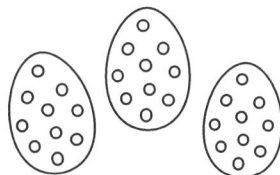

5

2

1

3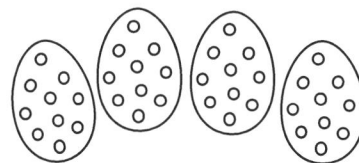

- BLANK PAGE -
left for bleed through

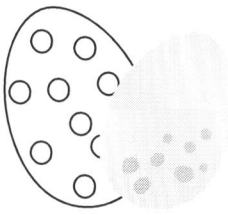

Cut, Paste and Color

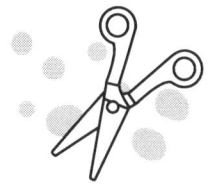

Cut out all the pieces. Paste them on the right place following the number. Color the picture.

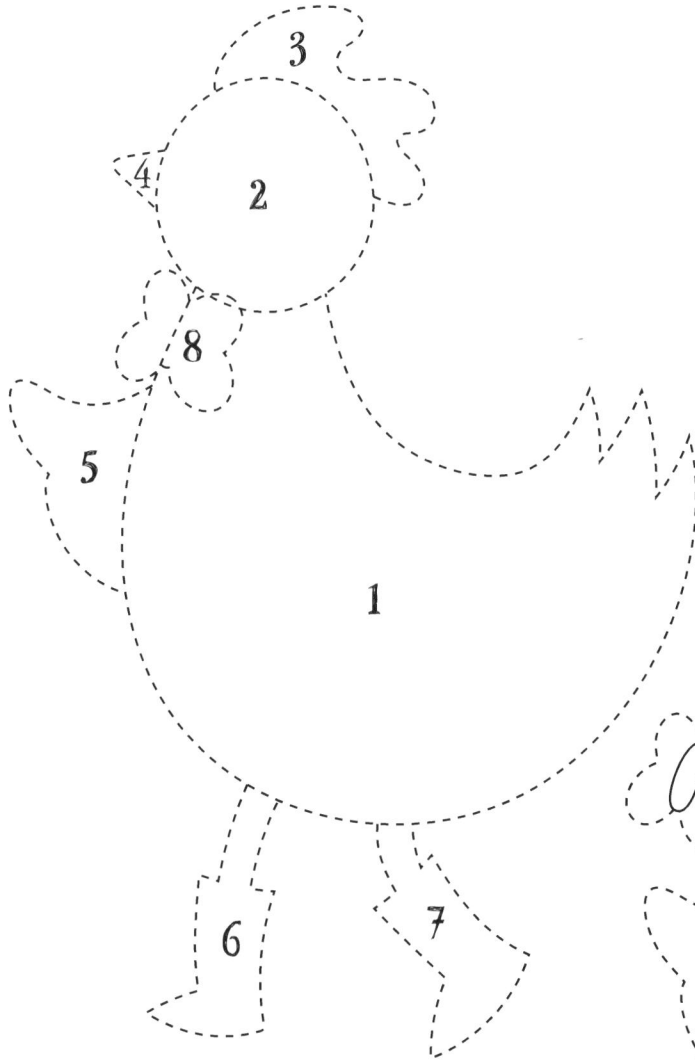

3

2

4

8

5

1

6

7

- BLANK PAGE -
left for bleed through

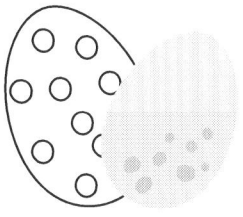

Easter Maze

Find the paths which lead to the carrots. Color the pictures.

- BLANK PAGE -
left for bleed through

Find the Diffrences

Find and circle 5 diffrences between the pictures.

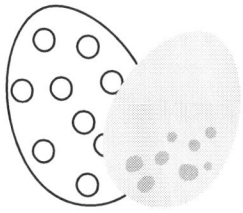

- BLANK PAGE -
left for bleed through

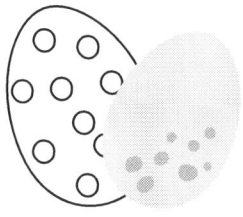

Easter Pattern

Color the pictures. Draw what comes next to continue the pattern.

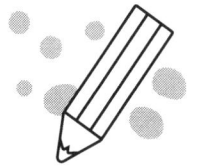

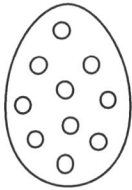

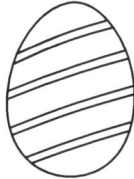

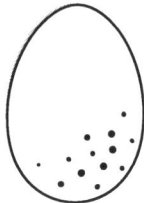

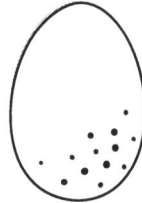

- BLANK PAGE -
left for bleed through

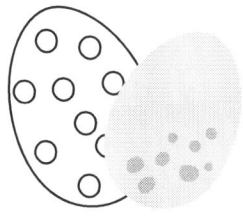

Shadow Matching

Draw a line from each object to its matching shadow.

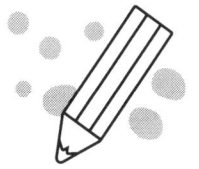

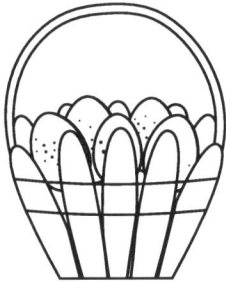

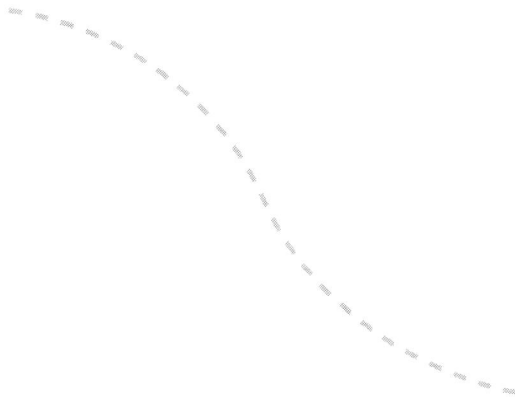

- BLANK PAGE -
left for bleed through

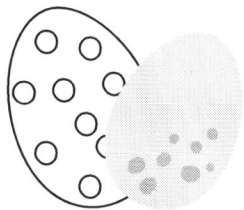

Drawing

Decorate Easter eggs. Color the pictures.

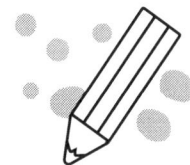

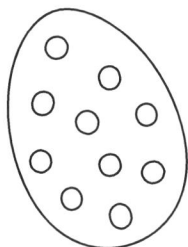

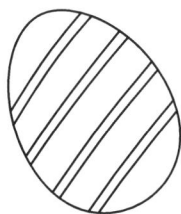

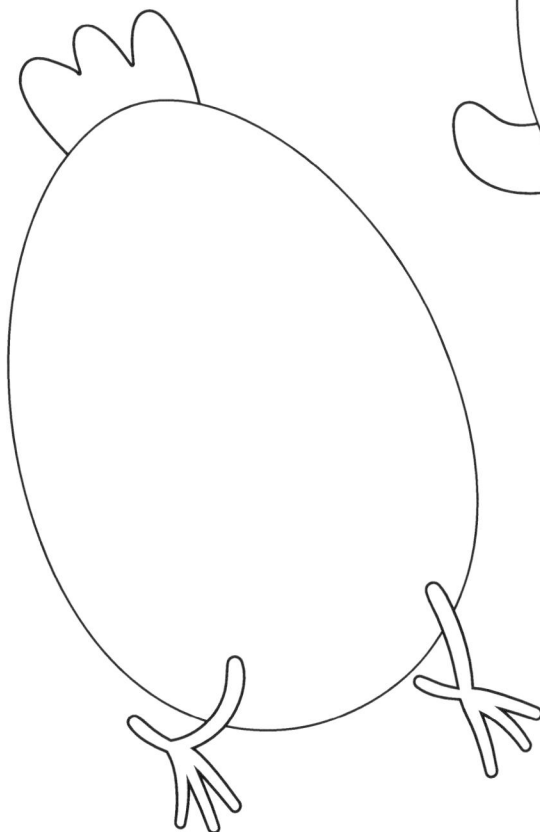

- BLANK PAGE -
left for bleed through

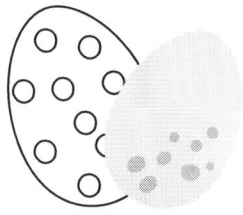

Finish the Picture

Finish drawing the picture. Color the picture.

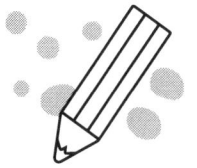

- BLANK PAGE -
left for bleed through

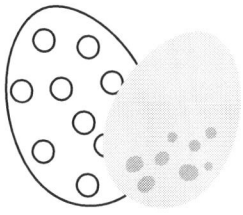

Line Tracing

Trace the lines. Color the picture.

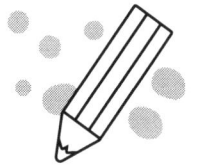

HAPPY
EASTER

- BLANK PAGE -
left for bleed through

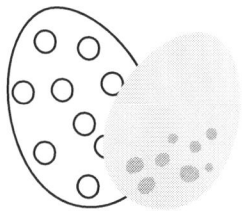

Easter Maze

Find what goes to the basket. Color the pictures.

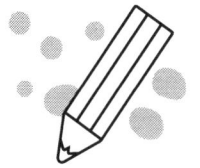

- BLANK PAGE -
left for bleed through

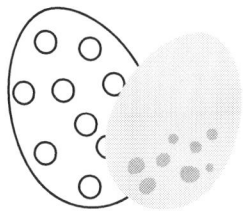

Line Tracing

Trace the lines. Color the picture.

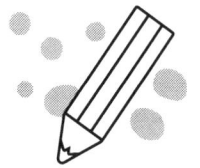

- BLANK PAGE -
left for bleed through

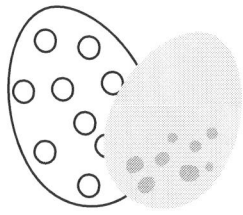

I Spy Easter

Write how many of these pictures you can find.
Color the pictures.

- BLANK PAGE -
left for bleed through

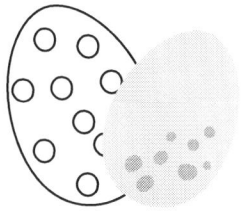

Easter Maze

Guide the Mother Bunny through the maze to her Baby.

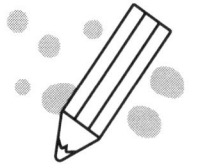

- BLANK PAGE -
left for bleed through

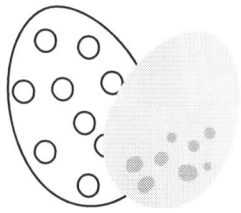

Find the Diffrences

Find and circle 5 diffrences between the pictures.

- BLANK PAGE -
left for bleed through

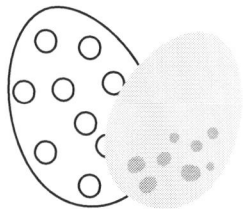

Line Tracing

Trace the lines. Color the eggs.

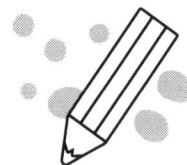

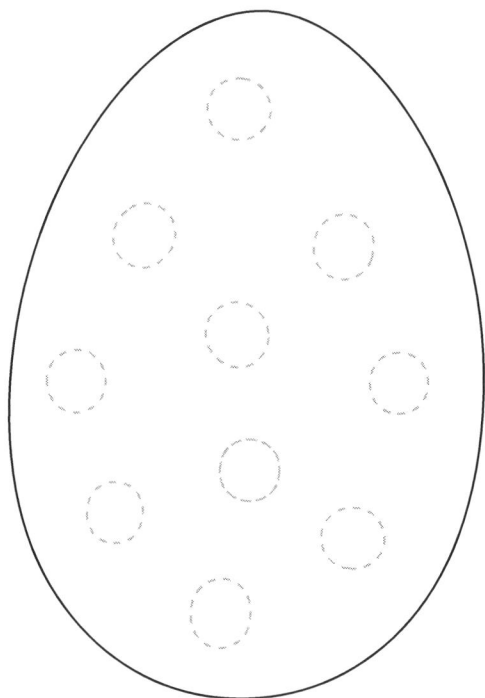

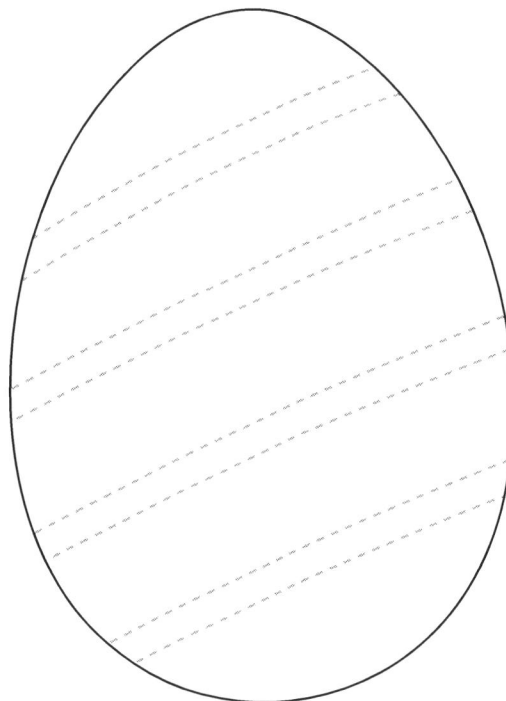

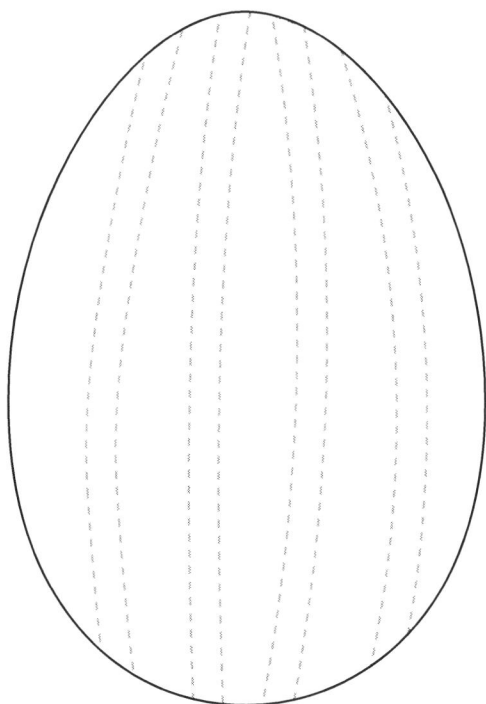

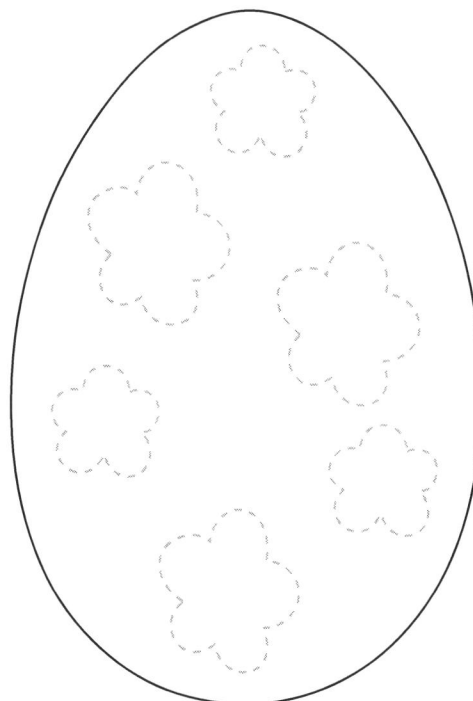

- BLANK PAGE -
left for bleed through

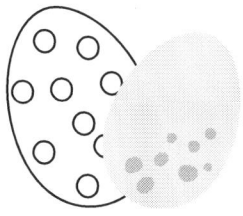

Connect the Dots

Connect the dots. Color the picture.

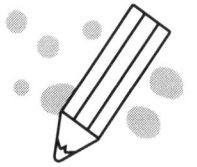

1
2
66
3
4
62
61   65
5
63
64
6
60   7
56   57
8
55   59
58 59
9
54
10
53
11
52
12
51
13
50
14
49
15
48
16
45   46   47
17
44
18
43
19
42
20
41 40
21
39
22
38
23
37
24   25
36   35
26
34   33   32   31   30   27
28
29

- BLANK PAGE -
left for bleed through

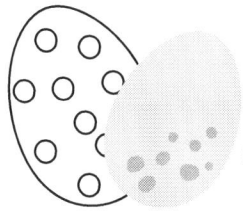

Tic Tac Toe

Color the markers, cut them out. Play the game with a partner.
The first player to get three in a row wins.

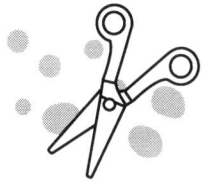

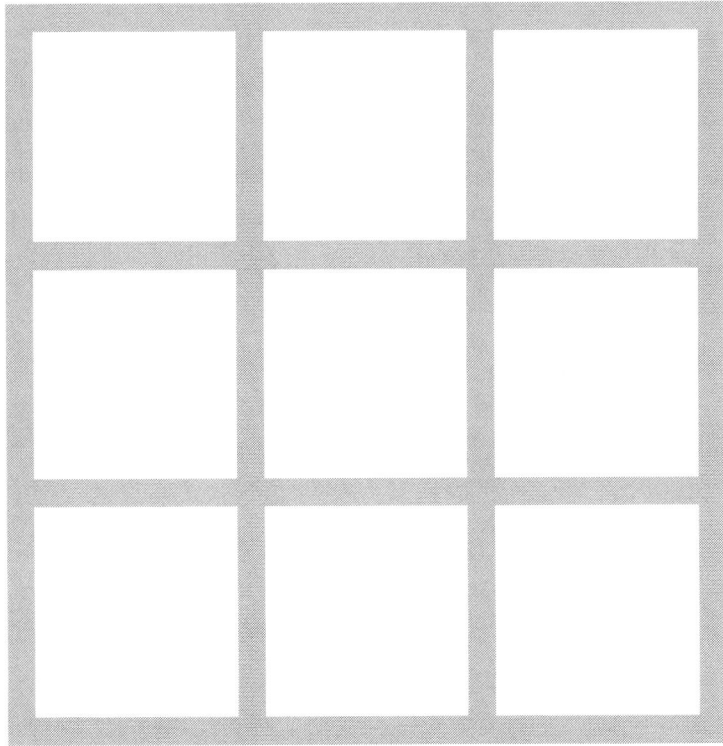

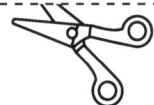

- BLANK PAGE -
left for bleed through

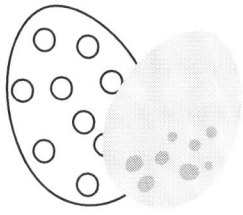

Easter Race

Two player game. Two game pieces and one dice needed.
The first player on the finish line wins the game.

- BLANK PAGE -
left for bleed through

Certificate

Presented To:

....

Congratulations! You did a brilliant job
of helping the Bunny family with Easter preparations.

Date:

Signed: Bunny Family

- BLANK PAGE -
left for bleed through

Made in United States
Orlando, FL
13 April 2022